THE BLACK BEACH

Previous Winners of the Vassar Miller Prize in Poetry
Scott Cairns, Series Editor

The Black Beach

Poems by J. T. Barbarese

2004 Winner, Vassar Miller Prize in Poetry

University of North Texas Press
Denton, Texas

10   9   8   7   6   5   4   3   2   1

Permissions:
University of North Texas Press
P.O. Box 311336
Denton, TX 76203-1336

The paper used in this book meets the minimum requirements of the
American National Standard for Permanence of Paper for Printed Library
Materials, z39.48.1984. Binding materials have been chosen
for durability.

Library of Congress Cataloging-in-Publication Data

Barbarese, J.T.
  The black beach : poems / by J.T. Barbarese.
    p. cm. – (Vassar Miller prize in poetry series ; no. 12)
  "2004 Winner, Vassar Miller prize in poetry ."
  ISBN 1-57441-188-8 (pbk. : alk. paper)
  I. Title. II. Series.
  PS3552.A59178B57 2005
  811'.54–dc22

                                    2004020731

The Black Beach is Number 12 in the Vassar Miller Prize in Poetry Series

Image on the cover is of the Three Pillars, photo by NASA

Design by Angela Schmitt

For Nico

Contents

III

Acknowledgments

The author would like to thank the editors of the following publications where these poems appeared, some in earlier versions.

The Atlantic: "Teaching the Slider"
Boulevard: "Walk Your Body Down" (under the title "The Couple to the Left of Me"), "Politics," "This," "Carapace," "Trying to be Penitent"
The Cortland Review: "Joy"
Denver Quarterly: "Elegy for L.J.B.," "Spinoza," "Pity," "Dream-Talking with General Massoud"
Georgia Review: "Suddenly," "Sea-Wrack Religion," "Hearing Roy Orbison on the Tape Loop at Starbucks," "Today on Sports Radio WIP"
Poetry: "The Landscape Wants to be Understood Slowly," "The Leaf on the Nursery Floor," "The Merman." Poems ©2004 The Poetry Foundation, reprinted by permission of the editor.
The Progressive: "On the 7-Something to Penn Station"
The Southern Review: "Memorial Day" (under the title "Labor Day: Tall Trees' Creaking")
Tiferet: "The Lost Beatitudes"
Washington Square: "Cities of God"

Walk Your Body Down

The couple on the left of me
is breaking up, the baby
on the ramp beside us
sings maniacally,
and a middle-aged black guy comes walking
down the center of the street,
and he looks rather like me—average build,
gathered into himself like an Arctic bird,
his aloneness at home here,
aloof as an element
yet who but he would care,
alone as earth or air
he knows nobody else is like him anywhere,

nothing is more memorable than ourselves.
Look at the way he stutter-steps down the center line,
look at the way he strides, as if to say,
walk your body proudly into the twilight
past that budded arrangement of sun and cloud,
past caskets of neighborhoods,
and all you remember, care for, is yourself
up to the moment when the mind leaves the curb in its black cab

and the conversations break up, and the people too,
and manic children sing on, in their minds still immortal,
and so is their pain
hurled up and down the ramp where the babies go up and down
like physics experiments
o, walk your body down, don't let it go it alone.

During

the first three weeks of March
everything was momentous.
Even odors had feast days,
there were shrines everywhere,
the city was my cathedral,
my ideas sutured the lives of the world's strangers,
each day was clay I ribbed and disciplined
and taught to speak,
but now that's done.
No sheep sleep where the butane tanks
rest sleek in the black sun.

The sharp-looking chesty woman with the nose-cone knees
still bends my way, still
loves my brute mind,
is still leaving her husband for me
but now and then stares savagely
like the audience at a crucifixion
hissing under its breath, *Come on
one more miracle*.

Onward

When he leaves in the morning
backpack half his height

Duke cap a compass needle,
coatless, this cold spring,

who knows if I'll see him again?
Love, the new world

is just like the old, only dumber.
The old symbols

(sun yolks on windows,
the early spring trees

snow-stripped, combative)
lack assurance,

seem diddled, washed-up,
and all the new stories

are wordless. But lots
of pictures. Distances cobbled

with smoke, flame paracletes
over retreating heads, spunk of fire

tipping cannons and faces,
while the middle-class hump it to school

like Sherpas, gravid with books,
curricula, syllabi, maps,

backward caps pointing the way:
bedeviled, onward.

Memorial Day

The tall trees creak like rockers and fill the park
with nursing-home sounds; they creak in mid-sentence,

break into the soft tacking of barbecue flames
over dogs and burgers, and fill me with baffled terror.

I wonder if all the dead had this recognition—
the sun going down on their borders, food warm in their bellies—

of flesh as a major protein, of the world as a meat locker?
Maybe God is a teenager totally into her body,

like one of those kids in the distance, taking her world
for a walk into the long continuous darkness

to "find herself," and lose it. Maybe the world is a creature
let run once into the wilderness between itself

and whatever it was that raised it into itself
and so lost it's forgotten it's lost, and looking for meaning

the way radio waves sought Marconi. While the flies sing
and cruise the waxed paper, while the winds

blacken in the smoke of food burning on the grill,
while everything here pretends it goes on forever,

let the girl with the hard hands and beautiful, lost walk
take her beauty off its leash, have it run ahead of her,

let us examine the tragedy of the last things
and the first things and the things unnumbered

or lost while the tall pines' creaking
keeps us running after the beauty that runs off without us.

Teaching the Slider

In the middle of life's road, which I notice
keeps getting wider,

he asks me to show him a slider.
Bankrupt, filled with rage, and now caught

on the phone with a merciful woman who isn't his mother,
I slam the phone down,

order him to the backyard,
and pitch. *Don't push off, separate*

because it's how you separate yourself from the mound,
it's all in the follow-through.

I come straight over the top.
They break smoothly, cleanly.

Once I broke them off and they fell
like knives outlining my victims.

Baseball's a game played sideways, I say.
He tries, is all legs and arms. His hands

half the span of mine, sneaks untied,
he's a present coming unwrapped. *No,*

you're not coming all the way through.
You need to fall through your body

as if it weren't there. You need to plunge
down the steps your legs and back make

and then the ball will break
and fall off the end of the world

no matter what and after that
your body can burst into flames

for all I care and I come through
and the ball cracks his glove, knocks it off.

He picks up my hand, turns my fingers,
touches my face, horrified.

He says he wants me to show him again
how I fall through my body

only this time, burst into flames.

Trying to Be Penitent

on the leather pews,
the wood was coming through,
so I thought only of my knees,
not his heroic finish
hammered to his handiwork,
not of the gory suds
that according to the sermoner
rivered from
his sacred liver

and ran downhill
into the mob that
was there to see God die
and on the under-card
the two common thieves
he hung between,
his arms extended like a politician
or emcee—

just two village punks
like the guys I grew up with,
Crazy Harry
who set houses on fire,
Barbone, who unsnugged
lug nuts and watched the cars
fall off their tires,
or the Jimmy Love that I
hung on the Poe School fence
for swiping my glove.
Glum and unrepentant,
even after he gave in
I kept beating him.

The censors snuffed,
I heard the *Ite, missa est*
and along with the rest
of the thoughtless and quick-heeled
rushed to the doors, sun-framed,
thanking the empty sky
that I would not that day
be with Him in Paradise.

Politics

(*Eau sourcilleuse*—Valéry)

Right after you're punched in the throat, begging for breath,
left there winded or broken, your jacket torn, change

glittering like spring rain all over the asphalt,
your umbrella in half, your books and testaments scattered,

your wallet spread in your hand like a dead canary,
dispossessed, you realize dispossession

is the lesson you've never been taught, have never taught.
You accept the new order: there are no rules.

Not even the book that says there are no rules,
— that there is no *you,* even — the book that, falling, flew up

and sits like a roof of a barn blown off in a storm,
not even that book is yours, not even the *langue*

aswim in the rant that comes out of your mouth instead of
paroles is yours. Not really. You are on your back,

there is nobody anywhere like you, and yet you are down,
whoever you are (or were), and as you are stomped

you see yourself. A man winterizing his car
half a block away. A kid half out a window.

A traffic light stuck on yellow. Overhead
a little white glittery whatsis sails west over rooftops

Baudelaire compared, once, to waves, and Paul Valéry
to something else. Eyes, maybe. Or was it eyebrows.

On the 7-Something to Penn Station

We walk up to the station. Kids already there
snack on the platform, half-eaten morning pastry
in their hands, schoolbags all over. My kid taps me
with a stick-on earring squeezed onto a toothpaste cap
she finds between the train seats. Says it's a thimble,
says make sure it doesn't get lost. It's important.
I start to tell her the truth but say sure, give it here,
and quietly lose it. The 7-Something pulls away
and ratchets east. Sunrise. I keep thinking of her
not able to sleep last night. Sitting up in her bed
and trying to count all the stars. The car swivels
and blinded I see them raised on their fathers' backs.
Not to be carried to bed. To breathe. Puddled feces
on the plank floor, stale breath, people saying prayers.
The boxcar lurches. There is no place to sit. No toilets,
so they piss where they are, holding whatever they took,
dark teddies, fouled dolls. Sitting high up in the dark,
watching the lights on their retinas. Make-believe stars,
they count them. They cannot breathe. They cannot sleep.

Today on Sports Radio WIP

the question of God's existence came up
because one of the personalities had just come
from the funeral of a good friend who had died suddenly.
He said he needed to talk it out. Forgotten were the Eagles
breaking camp in seven days, the Trotter giveaway,
the Flyers' new head coach, the Sixers
exiting in the first round, or the Phils'
loss to the Mets last night, a 1–0
classic pitchers' duel.
For a solid couple-three hours nobody mentioned
the Piazza rumor, or how Shawn Held went 6-for-6
and set a new record for single-game runs scored,
or that Heather Mitts, striker and mid-fielder
for the local women's soccer team
had posed half-naked on the cover of *Philly Mag*,
or the local woman just released from Holmesburg
after doing two years for trying to kill her husband
with "a fatal dose of mashed potatoes."

The Metaphysical ruled,
discourse was of divinity, God's existence.

Next up the dial a preacher was calling on God
to kill the new Herods who slaughter the innocent.
He read from Paul's Epistle to the Galatians.
On 1210, conservative Christians
pumped rhetorical iron, talked glory,
annihilation of nations. At the very end of the dial
the static that never signs off
swished, swept past. The song of the cosmic rays
that crash the Van Allen belt,
singing heat-death and birth,
all-enduring night.

Paper, Scissors, Rock

They might be seen arguing
in the park, shooting fingers:
paper, scissors, rock.

They hate their license pictures,
lose their keys, curse their kids, drink beer.
Walk dogs, pay taxes, read email.

They hate changing diapers,
like Bugs Bunny cartoons, quote films,
play cards, make phone calls.

They shop for clothes.
They strap things on,
they straighten, pose.

Their rage is a short blood shower.
Junk from the basement.
Ball bearings, dead 9-volts, a shot glass,

chipped Flintstones paperweight.
Dried finger. A stick, you think?
Glass fused to metal. Brain?
Brain aspic. Blood omelet. Bone toast.

The Prophet

wore a Boomer Esiason #7 Jets jersey over faded pre-washed jeans
belted with a length of ribbon he pulled out of the trash of Strings
and Things.

The sporting goods store gave him the jersey, a non-mover, the
year Esiason
signed as a free agent and stayed for a million-dollar cup of coffee.

He too had been passing through.
He wore a light gray cap and sneakers, smoked what he could bum,

needed a shave. Beard sloppy, a long Van Winkle.
Once in a while he would eyeball a pedestrian,

usually an older man heading to the cheese store
or up the avenue. Line him up and

har-har-har. An aristocratic bark, hard, farty.
The kids at the coffee bar let him hang out, gave him freebees.

There was his great stench. The things written on napkins.
Sidelined because of misery,

trying to ride a camel up the Space Needle.
One of the savvier baristas

(he had lectured her on her piercings)
called him the advance scout for the unemployed.

The morning of the day it began

she saw him crying into his hands on the bench outside,
came out and said Laddy, what's up.

Today is the Feast of St. Joseph, he said, blinking tears,
patron of them who go along. Then he got to his feet,

stood up and blew the store a kiss. *I will arise and go along.*
He has not come back.

Elegy

("...and his dying hour was gloom." Hawthorne)

Suddenly, nostalgia is the mother of irony.
You notice how bug-thick the air is
on August 8th and how the hot breeze

tossing fruit-leaves at the screen isn't sweetened
by what it bears. It enters smelling of death,
in fact, of ripeness and will stay suspended

like a dissonant in the scale until you can live
with your own inconsequence,
have held your breath and seen it resolved

into its several fogs and the "taking hence
of your insignificance" even though you know
there is no way to measure significance

when nothing really counts. So let grief go,
dream of the rope-ladder bridge and the pinnacled fort
that points its rouged finger into tomorrow's

crayoned hills and guides you toward Part Two
where Anxiety falls in love, elopes with Compassion,
lives happily ever after and overtakes you

like a Pony Express rider with the shocking but great news
that your life, that guilty criminal thing
made out of raised voices, has abruptly been pardoned,

the whole thing was a mistake, and those drawings of graves
you've been making with a trembling hand—be done with them,
come back to Beanyville, lay down your sorrow

where the broken chassis rust. Like the breezes tonight
with their missiles of sweet yellow leaves
whose sighs go unrecognized, let your breath take nothing

from the stricken words that body them into the gloom.

Close Call in Valley Green

I knelt to see what was rotting.
Non-specific corruption,
webbed and hammocked with cocoons,
maggoty. A bug bourse.
No telling what. Wren, robin,
winged rot. Gore had glued it
to shat-on grass. It was half-thawed
and I was filled with myself
and thought how beautiful,
the hard frost had cemented
what had lived to what never did,
then winter broke it and March warmed it
for me who knelt to it.

I got up, jittery. The Wissahickon
percolated down the ridge
uncontainable and bright
and eating at its banks. Above
the sun and sky
as lost in each other as blind dates;
and from the firs some nameless thing
sang four notes of a song
I thought I recognized,
and mouthed the lyrics;

but no. Mind is the only miracle,
the rest is the corpse it raised.
I kicked my *eureka* over the bridge,
scraped off the shit and hiked back to order,
straight streets, cops, chained city dogs.

The Merman

(for Nico)

The ripples on your wall:
fake sea-lights the soft sunlight makes.

You sleep under water.
Learn to love the counterfeit

and in the mess of shalts and shoulds and musts
find what you want.

Don't forget: I once stood loving
what was not here.

Number 99, Brian Santoro

a huge kid who played first base
hit Nico's third pitch straight into
a wind gusting from center

and it stayed up there. That wind banged it around
and Ryan caught it three steps
past the second base bag. It seemed a lock

that Santoro would make the fence, at least
deep center! Instead, it barely cleared the infield.
He stopped mid-trot, turned halfway to

first without hitting the bag, and his coach
looked away, mumbling. We
cheered Ryan, smiling at second,

and went on to win. They were already done.
It was only the third but the game
was greater than they,

even huge Brian Santoro, with his 99
like inverted tears on his back. I wanted to win
but even more wanted to know

what it was to be Brian Santoro,
after the wind sprang up
and said no through the puzzle-shaped clouds,

what it's like to be young and abruptly old,
an eleven-year-old Achilles, big-shouldered and doomed
and nameless, slouching into the rest of life.

Spinoza

(—*Deus, sive Natura.*)

He loved the northern sky and the fallen leaves
because men can do nothing to either.
There's nothing or something. Not both.
Things are not things but the clothes of change
and without change? Life is mere

practice. What is the everyday
that pulses and dies in you if there is
a sublimer? We live the hard undoing
of particulars.
God, the undoer that does.

Russell said his logic was flawless.
Nietzsche called him
greatest of philosophers. It comes down
to a single elegant inference:

There is no God. But if there were
(and this is his whole position—
inference based on a conjecture)
all that is must be God,
and there would be no need for priests or religions

since the only complete metaphysic
is a pantheism.

The hard part was explaining it,
this living as a thing in the world, a thing among things.
Something looks in on us as we look out
and makes for unhappiness. God the mother
that cannot refrain from doing, always doing.

When the Jews in the Hague
asked him what he believed
The proof of your foul disbelief, he replied,
then turned back to his grinding.

The Ones

hanging on corners.
That get kicked out of bars, out of houses, out of class

and never know you're talking to them.

That were riding one day on a school bus
when another kid grabbed their schoolbag and threw it

out the window into your neighborhood—
well lit, kid-thick, moms hanging out

on portables, dads cleaning gutters, checking their oil,
unfolding strollers. We might have picked it up,

given it one clean look before throwing it out.
That you think you know, you think you can get through to,

the ones to whom your life is the mansion
they enter and exit

as flies,
in one door, out another.

That can't be known. They are

a new theology, a new color. They are as here
as cold, pain, bone.

They are from the world's foundation.
Their God is ancient,

a hillbilly, unwashed, pissed off,
everywhere.

Poem in a Time of Infinite Justice

We are out here in the sunshine
last September Saturday
and everything marches
drumless, tragic, beautiful,

the toddlers, the derelicts, the busy hosts
that correspond to
our tolerable citizenry.
How many days can dazzle so

in one lifetime?
A life is twenty-six thousand days.
The best are unnumbered.
The colors stiffen and snap.

When we are no longer
someone must remember
that each of us marched
one Saturday in September

to his particular pounding heart.
The aircraft veed up beside the geese,
migrating idylls, marvelous illusion,
and the pregnant preceded their

husbands who followed their bellies
like wobbly towed rowboats.
Long-legged mythic beauties in shorts
walked back and forth

past the Ford showroom windows
like out-of-work goddesses
and between the traffic's pulses
you could hear the silence conspiring.

None of us seemed concerned
with the coming war in heaven
that we who fight the gods' battles
are men and women.

The Leaf on the Floor

*—Some leaves of a tree had been found on the nursery
floor.* J.M. Barrie.

Between fresh sheets,
they open their mouths,
gulp sleep.

The crunched springs
(windows up) sound
like cellos, tuning:

low, autumnal, worn.
It is a dry fall.
They feed their rooms

their sighs.
Things hit their marks
outside,

aircraft, crickets.
C-5s, big-bellied
with ordnance,

jump over the moon.
The cicada
resumes.

Their sighs run
to breath's edge, back.
Powdered and bathed,

snugged and tucked,
beloved
lie of continuity.

The door sucks shut.
One leaf—
palmed x-ray

of a day
(soccer fields,
victory, friends)—

descends:
stark animals,
dull sunsets,

blessings, meals, baths,
toweled and talcumed white
as plastered lath,

now I lay me,
do not slay me,
let me stay

alive,
alive,
asleep

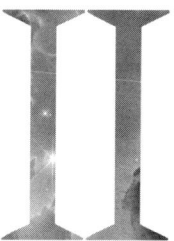

The finite, annihilated in the presence of the infinite.
—Pascal

Sea-Wrack Religion

I'm watching two dogs whistled back to their owner,
twin braids unbraiding up to the boardwalk,

but really came here to look at the damage—
the organic, the pigtailed sea-plants and the gutted shell,

the driftwood, the dead crab kebobbed with an ice cream spoon,
that empty horseshoe crab's carapace

tossed like a football helmet way up the beach,
the spindrift fuzz slicking clamshells and seaweed,

all of it picked over like a Labor Day sale
by terns and gulls and pigeons,

and all the while the mile-out breakers
running forever in place—

the logic of it! How it picks and factors,
this water-and-wind algorithm

working the beach, solving the rocks
into expressions not even remotely human.

We call this process god
because it is what we do—

the god we never see and that never sees us.

But the dogs, the dogs' helixing home over the dunes,
twisted and twinned—their parody of the eternal—

finally gets to me. The girl who is meeting them
is young and leggy, and her hands are so lit up

by the reflecting sea they flicker and fall
over the dogs like Pentecostal tongues.

Which of us lives forever? Which light is mine
in all the lights that swarm like blind sperm

around the brute moon, so self-possessed

it will never know what it was, so pure that it seems
that nothing, no human pain, can reach it again?

She extends her hands again, two more lights

among those spreading out all over the east,
and she'll never know my desire, and I'll never know hers.

Above us both, while her dogs run on ahead,
is the black beach of heaven where all desire
is merged, twinned, recovered, braided, and set ablaze.

This

This is where it all begins, the ant-feast,
the diet of worms,

the unsocketings and outflows.
The cardinal

kinked in the folded shade glows
like a new scab

and the star-starved sky looks down. Something
with dusk for pincers

steers its food down the tree
and the soil, a micaceous slick

of slug slime and dew, sighs *come*.
A gulp of sunlight and sight, the hole

takes, takes.
And the cardinal lectures

the scabbed shade
about emptiness.

Pity

My children will age and die,
along with the messenger who pedals by
and sweats through the shirt pocket where he stuffed
                                    his lunch money this morning
stained with his common stink,

and along with Mrs. Bugay, the jeweler's widow,
in her old dress and her hair kinked like cotton candy
                                    and tinted Confederate red,
working her way up the hill to her cozy shop,
one of the all-time great pedestrians, like Dante, but so old
she lifts her mouth like an open beggar's cup
for the sky to fill with air, she's so out of breath,

and the woman on the litmag cover, all educated cuteness
                                    I even pity her,
anointed a genius she carries that rep everywhere
like Hester dragging Pearl all over town,
and even with her prize money and two-hundred-dollar haircut,
and her stiff blue suit that makes her look like so butch,
still when she wakes up she remembers how it felt

to rise in the darkness and hear the rigs
rocking toward the city, the cars uncoupling,

the smell of cut sweetgrass, the silhouetted convoys,
to hear without seeing, to smell without tasting,

wondering who was taking, who being taken,
and seeing in the banded east a gift-wrapped dawn

and praying for her own first words, *let my words be mine.*

But most lives are pretty good voices that can't hit
                                    the high notes,

and ambition the lover who can't find the room key,
and in the hazel shadows crisscrossing the snow field
the sun lay exposed in its last lights, a molested thing

among the snow hills,
night coming on.

Poem to My Daughter on Her Eighteenth Birthday

"Henry pursued Louis VI
of France, his brother-in-law,
half-heartedly"—toying with him, really,
grabbing French provinces along the way—
"reducing the rebellious garrison of Domville
on his way back to Rouen
to strike at rebellious Harry, his son, the Prince,"
who would die young.
"Henry chased Louis as far as Fougéres on the coast,
a town in the North,"

and the name of the five-dollar
wine I finished the night you were born
and ripped your mother's womb as you entered the very same
light
that Fougéres, Henry Plantagenet, low-born Becket
(the first English saint), Geoffrey of Blois,
that hell-raiser Raymond of Toulouse
(the Ché of his century), that hell-cat Eleanor,
and the only English Pope, Alexander III,
occupied long before us. Their names and histories
are a sober ecstasy, like paid-off mortgages,

because you still lie in their future,
and I did not die young
but would toast your birth
with bloody Fougéres in a bright glass,
21 March 1985
eight hundred years after Henry slogged "through English mud
to avoid pitched battles" (he was actually
"sickened by violence"),
long after Becket's murder,
eight centuries distant from France, then a virgin frontier
from Toulouse to the Piedmont Plateau in Northern Italy,
home of my mother's father, your great-grandfather,
the ex-Jesuit, Army translator, flautist and Freemason,

who did die young.

Vision in the Flourtown Mall, Saturday

I will wander through these dollar stores
like a Saturday retiree,
the roads clogged because the evacuation
had run out of gas,
thousands stranded in SUVs with their brand new clutches and
bright August inspection stickers and crippled air conditioning,
each with $1000 in cash (or an equivalent) inside a sock
or underpants,
dead cell phones in pockets,
kids crying
windows rolled up against the poisons.

I'll watch from the empty mall parking lot
a couple of stragglers load up on double cheeseburgers
piled up on a sideboard, a door broken down,
abandoned pets wandering, one on a leash, sniffing
at something lost or tossed,
some locked up at home, dead flies at the bottom of
dried up water dishes,
the hot water heaters cold,
freezers hot,
grotesqueries of defrosted meat, melted ice cream,
dropped ceilings on floors,
fried VCRs, flooded basements, verminous second floors
and squirrelly porches,
the roads out abruptly impassable, all roads out,
the gas gone.

I'll wander the empty parking lots
and the malls,
stores with their protective grills pulled down,
some half-down, some pried up halfway.
A tee-shirt caught in the grill,
shattered joysticks outside Electronics Boutique,
useless DVDs VCRs XBoxes

sad remotes tragic antennae stark printers and fax machines,
a thousand replayable imaginary battles
in crushed Novalogic boxes on the shadowless pavements.

I'll head over to Auntie Anne's, grab a buttery pretzel.
I will say out loud Your money is no good here, sir.
The lemonade warm, pulpy, sweet,
a warm wind through the place, origins unknown,
puddles from burst return lines in front of the doorways
a moat around the information booth
a lone pigeon in a pool of Uncle Cho's chicken and water,
birds in the broken displays pecking the watches and collectible
baseball cards
signed bats and balls and fitted caps,
all that you can't take with you.
I'll open my wallet and unthread my last worthless dollar
and take a couple packs of Wrigley's for the long walk,
and leave the buck on the counter, say Keep the change,

and listen.

The Lost Beatitudes

Blessed are the sons-of-bitches
since that includes most of us.

Blessed are the Christians and Jews and all Fundamentalists
who remind us in the end that it's all about real estate.

Blessed are the religions without transcendence,
the Wiccans and Theosophists and Druids.

Blessed the middle-aged folk who jog to stay in shape,
sleek black shadows majestic in Spandex on gentle slopes.

Blessed are the nude and the nudists
for flesh is our precious illusion.

Blessed are the beautiful for beauty
is the decisive consolation.

Blessed are those who pine and pray for the Rapture,
for assuring me that I will be left behind.

Blessed are those seven-year-olds carrying their bleeding
                              cherry snow cones and s'mores
into Cineplexes and showrooms, singing out *wait up*
                              and tracking young filth over old
nothing ever waits,
great joy makes us shiver.

Blessed is the good-looking Marine with his good-looking wife
eating pizza on the sidewalk, each piece folded over,
not even twenty, with tall matching cheekbones and chestnut hair,
for the world is doomed and doesn't deserve them
yet they are radiant and abundant and optimistic.

Blessed are the two older women getting up from the table
and about to run to the Gap, leave a modest tip
                    and saying as they go
Under five dollars fifteen percent, over five it's like
                    twenty
for they are the world.

Blessed are Dante, Twain, Hart Crane and Emily Dickinson
and that cheap redhead with a mutt on a red leash
standing there like a smoldering trash fire,
and blessed is her mutt,
and blessed are all intentions, good ones and bad.

Blessed are flat-Earthers, Seventh Day Adventists and Scientologists,
and blessed the morning sun smudged in clouds
like a luminous toilet seat,
and that gorgeous brunette now striding across the street,
                              blessed be she,

just for showing up this morning,
this blessed morning.

Carapace

The world decays
around you, always,
and the rust crowds in.
The sun stokes the leaf,
the wind sucks the gutter,
and the firs lose their pins,

but it's also a shock to see
ladybugs blackened by rot,
the lipstick bodies frost-bit, unbright,
and realize they never knew
how lonely it was
even had they known what hit them,
or that when death arrived
they could no longer live.

It makes you a human being
that you do know this
standing on the ladder's top rung,
that you go on cleaning the gutter
then go on going on.

Suddenly

I'm sick of the careful ironies,
I look forward to the birds' broken English in the morning—
but how could I have forgotten their
ad-libbed *Angelus*
or the spider web's spokes of light
as the sunny rope of water runs down my body
and the dawn-whitened walls,
how could I have forgotten their
coincidental dawnsong when her lips
are pale as a clouded dawn
and patched with chapping,
when Nico's face whitens like the east and his white arms
reach out of his finite heat,
how ever could I have forgotten
that the sun throws my shadow behind me
like used negative and holds me up to the light
not as I always am, not as I should be, but as I am now?
That this is what I have lived for,
this is happiness,

no divine guarantors,
no God, no gods,
living in every inch of the body,
scene of all the life there is.

Holding My Face to My Son's Tee-Shirt

1.

Holding my son's tee-shirt to
my face I smell body heat
in the front. The back is damp and slicked
with his doggy sweat and the street's

paste of crankcase oil and leaves.
It has memorized his skin
and I hold it up like Veronica's
dark salvific napkin.

2.

Washed now, why see what I see:
vistas of flattened food malls,
children fetal in ditches
SWAT teams roaming the halls,

a righteous crank reloading,
shooting the splinted and split,
and a nine-year-old turtled up in his shirt
something bloodying it?

Hearing Roy Orbison on the Tape Loop at Starbucks

The 9th makes no difference to canyons,
and it was Mozart they played at the camps
over the roar, the oven hiss.
A couple years ago,
I was standing over the body of a dead bird,

and suddenly
some hallucinatory
cardinal piped the opening notes
of one of the Supremes' last hits.

What is the meaning of meaning to what
can't feel its own thought?

Pretty woman, talk to me
nel mezzo del camin',
tell me why you're here
so I'll know why I am,

sip the iced coffee,
lick the roof of your mouth
that will rot into un-feeling,
wear the dominant immobile brown,
the death uniform.

Poverty and what passes
is our music,
the self
subtracted from sense,
Hendrix under the dome of the dream,
Brahms on a red donkey bearing sticks and straws,

and the sublime Roy on the knoll overlooking
the valley where what never gets said
is buried like fish under water,
eyes in heads.

Three Prayers

—Pleni sunt coeli et terra et gloria Dominus.

Cantico del Sol:

The first robin of spring
dead on the lawn.

Vigilant crows overhead. Spiritless, hungry.
That woman in the house one up,

pregnant, her first, balloons
out her screen door, a small Big Bang.

Barefoot is spring. Bellying windows,
beds of old snow, egg-yolk of sun,

omnidirectional cloud-spread,
a scattered sheepfold, with a what-now look.

*

Gloria:

O God of wrathful resource, fierce mathematics,

of far off bunk-beds of clouds,
of fallen gutters, lost siding, dark snow,

of the dry wall men hang in their sleep,
and of dawn's dripping paint job

be with my Neighbor John, breaking in his new hip,
as he waves into the glare and speaks,

benign in his negritude, a shadow
peeled and peregrine and lost.

O God of the Void perpendicular
to the endless nothing,

Plentiful are the heavens and earth.
Birds on the line, two bars from an old score, go

silent suddenly. It reads *There is no God*.
The birds sing: *only light and shadow*.

*

Act of Contrition:

Full moon, taking aim
on our pervious roofs

we have taken out loans to fix them.
Each is a personal essay.

We have worked hard on them.
They have no theses,

begin and end wrongly,
lack all sense of audience

and come to you untitled,
without even names.

Some were collaborative,
and come uncontrite.

Allow us their protection.
Allow them to pass.

Dream-Talking with General Massoud

These are my brothers, he says nodding out the window. A jeep
idles outside. Two men leg-wrestle by a flattened soccer ball. He
tells me he was an indifferent athlete in the school he attended,
a French school. I tell him about baseball, that I coach baseball,
and I realize he looks like my youngest brother. I remind him of
someone too, an older man, a teacher he feared from his youth.
We are in a room with smudged walls and blackened floor, and
there's a window to my right. Two men arrive in the sunshine and
start talking to one of his soldiers. He sees me looking off and says
Men are here to interview me. I realize what day it is. Why are the
walls black? He says This is where I will be killed. He is smiling a
doomed aristocrat's smile, the smile of men not by nature smilers.
I tell him I refuse to fly, and yet I must have flown here. Did I?
Gentle doomed smile. Don't fly, he says, it's unnatural. From now
on, *run*. I realize what day it is. A gorgeous day, and the mountains
are tight and blue and muscular in the windows. I squint to see
him disappear around the smudged building and reappear. He
greets the strange men who will kill him in this room where he
has already been killed. He is the Tajik Massoud, the Lion of the
Panjshir, who hated to kill but excelled at combat. His teacup is
filled with salt water. There are dry leaves all over the floor. There
is a ball in the far corner covered with fruit leaves. There are no
trees, anywhere. There are no soccer fields. Somebody comes in
and says He cannot see you tomorrow, he will see you now.

Joy

sometimes shows up where nothing was
the way wildflowers will
suddenly be where nothing was
on the banks of highway hills

for some over-the-road truck driver,
who happens to sort of half-look
past the angles of his fingernails
down the cover of the matchbook

between his teeth, then asks himself
What's up with that old field
and feels his lonely surprised heart
shaken, and maybe healed.

The Landscape Wants to be Understood Slowly

The ripples processing
from here then gone
beyond the pool
into distant gorge
and damp sand are
not mine but oh
how they remind
me—each
in widening flight
from origins
—that so much
is kept from me,

how the stoppered sap sticks
where the bark bled
over the stumps, so that
once frost smites the ground
a rich rice of maggots
will freeze to the peach
(that, falling, froze
to the trashcan lid).

Bless this world's cold economies,
its fat snowed-in violence.
July's bonanzas end
in a rot-hollowed stump:

that such bogus integrity throve
in the green heart of void.

A Noise of Crows

and it's day,
the light just about level with the edges
of the neighborhood
as if God has trouble
staying in the margins,

but it's day.
Flies hymn to the dogshit,
the clouds pause by the sun
like guests too awed to come in.
Even the mulch piles sing,
a bird seems lost in a reflection
it does not know is its own
and though the radio warns me that
everyone but me is getting rich

it's day, and morning
out of its own blue nothing is building noon.

Cities of God

Just as I head into the turn at the curve
below the regatta stands and not a mile above

Boathouse Row and the emergent trees
and the geese on the river bank unfazed by the city-borne traffic,

it scallops up—the cathedral's sky-blinking dome,
unblinking blue tile

sky-tilting, eyeballing heaven,
then rectangled in rear view mirror

and lost in the tree line, fall-gilt and -greened
and gone. The glare on the windshield is a manic

daylight mosaic, and I feel sick with light
and of all the life there is and that I have only one,

of all you have to do before you are done,
of the life I leave behind, like one of those high-rises

stalled in mid-construction,
startled ideogram, a tangle of scaffold.

Then it's behind me, to remind me—with the sole trace of closure
the day's origami gone crazy on all the windows—

how the sun throws its red rigging up from the east
and derricks the work-thick day and builds new projects

for workers to park themselves, to hang up their keys and umbrellas,
to shut their eyes on the city of the Self, gone silent.

Anisette

(for Simone)

Bianca with saddlebags of fat
and Marge with half a cataract
work the loaves of gnocchi dough.
Where the sweat sticks, flour snow-caps
brows and eyelids. Cousin JoJo kisses
cousin Rita's mouth in the bushes
in back of the house between the cyclone
fence and the roses. Inside, Uncle Pep
counts face cards, cusses the pot,
all nickels, dimes and crumbs, then
covers his hand when coffee is poured,
uncorks the anisette, looking off
to the back of the house: the rose-plaited fence
stirs in a smother of shadows.
God's windless sunshine. Uncle Lou dumps
a fifth sugar into his cup. He adds a shot
of anisette, pours one for Pep, *salut*
and knocks it back. He spreads his cards
into a victory fan. Overhead
children storm down a hallway, all
sixty feet of the house, stop, storm back.
Uncle Pep doesn't look up. *Turks*,
he says. *I'm pat.* Two more children,
Frankie's boys, duel with palm strands
blessed at Easter morning mass. Luke and Darth,
their fronds light-swords. Their mother folds
linen napkins and notices
the shaking roses and wonders
where Frankie is. He is out front
in the staling sunshine, his coat off,
his head under the hood checking his oil
while dolled-up parishioners
file home from mass, high hair puffed
stiff with spraynet. He smokes,
greased fingernails blacking his cigarette,

ash snowing on his suit pants. He smells
the spring under the asphalt and gas
and antifreeze. The white flowers,
that bursting tang. He likes spring
but prefers motors. In the side mirror
he can see JoJo pressing Rita into
the chain-link fence. The roses bob.
He remembers the sharp pinch
of cold fence between his fingers
as he gripped and rode. He sips his cigarette
like drink. He cannot *not* look
at his resurrected self. The fabulous sameness
and its vague differences, measured
like engine tolerances in pregnancies, kids, deaths.
He twirls his wedding band. Inside
the uncles are twirling their wedding bands
and losing money. The sun strokes its gold
as it twirls, light coming back
in winking wheels. Upstairs the kids
queue up on the landing and come down
hand over hand, head first. The aunts
below are working wordlessly,
pounding and kneading, in a blizzard
of drizzled flour. When their sweat
in clear salt beads falls on the dough
they fold it in. It is more food.
Flushed up against the fence,
Rita feels his warm beard under her chin
and the cold fence down her back.
I love you, he says. She feeds him herself
lips, tongue—and breathes his breath:
anisette, provolone, cigarettes, all JoJo's
worldly promise, the argument
she has been waiting to lose.
I love you, she says. First giggling,
then not. Against the hard links
hands crushed, twined. Cold, she thinks.
Then, white gold, red gold, cold gold.